D1420400

YOU'RE THE BEST

summersdale

YOU'RE THE BEST

Compiled by Peggy Jones

An Hachette UK Company
www.hachette.co.uk

Summersdale Publishers Ltd
Part of Octopus Publishing Group Limited
Carmelite House
50 Victoria Embankment
LONDON
EC4Y 0DZ
UK

www.summersdale.com

Printed and bound in China

ISBN: 978-1-80007-702-7

Substantial discounts on bulk quantities of Summersdale books are available to corporations, professional associations and other organizations. For details contact general enquiries: telephone: +44 (0) 1243 771107 or email: enquiries@summersdale.com.

To..

From......................................

I am deliberate
and afraid of
nothing.

Audre Lorde

Own your energy

You can, you should,
and if you're brave
enough to start,
you will.

Stephen King

YOU'RE MORE THAN ENOUGH.

Olivia Rodrigo

KICK
SOME
ASS

As soon as you trust yourself, you will know how to live.

Johann Wolfgang von Goethe

My courage always rises at every attempt to intimidate me.

Jane Austen

Do you know how incredible you are?

With confidence, you have won before you have started.

Marcus Garvey

Eventually it comes
to you: the thing
that makes you
exceptional.

Lorraine Hansberry

Never
apologize
for who
you are

Channel the best part of you that is bigger than yourself.

Ethan Hawke

You can go
forth and make
this world a
better place.

Bill Nye

YOU
ALREADY
HAVE SO
MUCH TO BE
PROUD OF

**Don't give up.
Don't turn off
your light.**

Chris Witherspoon

Try to be a rainbow in someone's cloud.

Maya Angelou

YOUR TIME
IS NOW

The moment we
decide to fulfil
something, we can
do anything.

Greta Thunberg

What is done in love is well done.

Vincent Van Gogh

Grab
that
dream

Never bend your
head. Always hold
it high. Look the
world straight
in the eye.

Helen Keller

CELEBRATE
YOURSELF.

Ariana Grande

CREATE
YOUR OWN
SUPPLY OF
INSPIRATION
AND IT'LL
NEVER
RUN DRY

Accept no one's definition of your life, but define yourself.

Harvey Fierstein

Ignore the naysayers.

Chris Pine

Trust
yourself

If you have
the ability to love,
love yourself first.

Charles Bukowski

Love yourself
unconditionally,
just as you love
those closest
to you despite
their faults.

Les Brown

Go
get it

Your originality is what makes you stand out.

Bretman Rock

When you have
exhausted all
possibilities,
remember this:
you haven't.

Thomas Edison

LIVE WHAT YOU BELIEVE, AND BELIEVE WHAT YOU LIVE

Action is the antidote to despair.

Joan Baez

You are what
you believe
yourself
to be.

Paulo Coelho

YOU
AMAZE
ME EVERY
DAY

In your own life
it's important
to know how
spectacular
you are.

Steve Maraboli

What you have inside is much more beautiful than what's on the outside.

Selena Gomez

Dream it, then do it

You can do
whatever you
really love to
do, no matter
what it is.

Ryan Gosling

I RUN MY WORLD.

Beyoncé

YOU'RE
WINNING

It's about listening to yourself and truly knowing what makes you happy.

Lea Michele

Be bold.
If you're going
to make an error,
make a doozy.

Billie Jean King

Write your own script, then enjoy the show

Look inside yourself and find your own inner strength.

Mariah Carey

Always be a
first-rate version
of yourself, instead
of a second-rate
version of
somebody else.

Judy Garland

Do
what
you do
best

You get one life. Who cares what everyone else thinks?

Kelly Clarkson

If your world
doesn't allow you
to dream, move to
one where you can.

Billy Idol

MAKE YOUR MOVE

Your perspective is unique. It's important and it counts.

Glenn Close

Vitality shows not only in the ability to persist but in the ability to start over.

F. Scott Fitzgerald

NOBODY COMPARES TO YOU

When you get to
the end of your
rope, tie a knot
and hang on.
And swing!

Leo Buscaglia

You are not your past. You are prepared for your future.

Karamo Brown

Be yourself and you can't go wrong

The world
belongs to
the energetic.

Ralph Waldo Emerson

ALL GLORY COMES FROM DARING TO BEGIN.

Eugene Fitch Ware

ACCEPT
YOUR
WHOLE
SELF

I'm not stopping.
I think maybe
that's my best
quality.

Cher

Be happy for this moment. This moment is your life.

Omar Khayyam

You are
entitled to
all the joy
you can
imagine

Speak your mind, even if your voice shakes.

Maggie Kuhn

Stand firm
and stay
consistent.

Solange

There is so much power and possibility within you

I always
feel confident.
I never allow
myself to not
feel confident.

Amber Rose

You decide
what you are,
what you want
to express.

Gianni Versace

RADIATE, SHINE, GLOW

I am not going to be silent.

Madeleine Albright

No one else can ever be you.

Pink

COMPARE YOURSELF TO NO ONE

Always be
yourself:
express yourself,
have faith in
yourself.

Bruce Lee

Do what you want to do.

Harry Styles

Wear your crown with pride

Say yes to life,
and embrace it
wherever
it is found.

James Baldwin

I AM SURE OF MYSELF AS A PERSON.

Dolly Parton

KEEP ON
ROCKING

You are your best thing.

Toni Morrison

Learn more about yourself and fall more in love with yourself every day.

Zendaya

Tomorrow's
going to be
even better

Get to the deeper business of being beautiful inside.

Lupita Nyong'o

The big lesson in
life, baby, is never
be scared of anyone
or anything.

Frank Sinatra

Be completely and perfectly you

Put your shoulders back and chin up, and face the world with pride.

Helen Mirren

Believe in your
heart what you know
to be true about
yourself.

Mary J. Blige

YOU'VE GOT NOTHING TO PROVE

Do your little bit of good where you are.

Desmond Tutu

Find your own style and have the courage to stick to it.

Joan Crawford

BEING
AMAZING
DOESN'T
MEAN BEING
PERFECT

Value yourself
and know that
you're worth
everything.

Jennifer Lopez

There are
darknesses in
life and there
are lights,
and you are
one of the lights.

Bram Stoker

Nothing wrong with being a little extra

I'm strong,
I'm powerful and
I'm confident.

Serena Williams

JUST BE
YOU.

Joe Locke

KEEP
CLIMBING

Just do it and eventually the confidence will follow.

Carrie Fisher

Nobody can tell me what I can and cannot do.

Amna Al Haddad

Go all
in on your
dreams

I don't need to be like anyone else but myself.

Doja Cat

I am not an angel,
and I will not be
one till I die:
I will be myself.

Charlotte Brontë

Confident, self-assured, flourishing

You're always with yourself, so you might as well enjoy the company.

Diane von Fürstenberg

The minute you
learn to love
yourself you
won't want to
be anyone else.

Rihanna

KEEP THAT
HEAD UP

I am stronger than I am broken.

Roxane Gay

**Be yourself
and people
will like you.**

Jeff Kinney

YOU ARE
WORTHY
OF IT ALL

Be yourself.
The world worships
the original.

Ingrid Bergman

You are
beautiful,
and you
can do
anything.

Lizzo

Your
peace is
precious

You're smart
and talented
and accomplished
and perfect
just the way
you are.

Rebel Wilson

BE YOUR BEST SELF CONSTANTLY.

Indya Moore

WHAT BELONGS TO YOU WILL FIND YOU

I was made exactly the way I was meant to be made.

Megan Rapinoe

Never dull your shine for somebody else.

Tyra Banks

Keep
that energy
flowing

Stay true to your principles, live passionately and fully and well.

David Nicholls

At the end
of the day I'm
just doing me.

Lil Nas X

Right now is a great time to be you

To love oneself is the beginning of a lifelong romance.

Oscar Wilde

The main person
you have to trick
into confidence
is yourself.

Zadie Smith

YOU
ROCK

**Have fun
and do what
you love.**

Yasmin Finney

You don't have to become something you're not to be better than you were.

Sidney Poitier

SHOW
NO
FEAR

Those who bring
sunshine into the
lives of others
cannot keep it
from themselves.

J. M. Barrie

**Be confident.
Be loud.
Say what you
wanna say.**

Willow Smith

You're
the
baddest

Life isn't about
finding yourself.
Life is about
creating yourself.

George Bernard Shaw

WHAT
I AM IS
BRAVE.

Lucille Ball

BE BRAVE
AND LISTEN
TO YOUR
HEART

I'm beautiful no matter what.

Demi Lovato

Say yes, and you'll figure it out afterward.

Tina Fey

Take all
the time
you need

Resist much,
obey little.

Walt Whitman

Be happy
with the
beautiful
things that
make you, you.

Beyoncé

Your
future
begins
here

Go confidently in the direction of your dreams.

Henry David Thoreau

The greatest
mistake you can
make in life is
to be continually
fearing that you'll
make one.

Elbert Hubbard

SAVE SOME LOVE FOR YOURSELF

You are
not alone.

Kurt Vonnegut

I'm not afraid of anybody.

Priyanka Chopra

REFUSE
TO LOSE

You are
beautiful.

Ariel Winter

If you'll just stand up and go, life will open up for you.

Tina Turner

Turn and face the sunshine

I can't go back
to yesterday
because I was
a different
person then.

Lewis Carroll

AUTHENTICALLY
ME
AS I CAN BE.

Shea Couleé

YOUR POTENTIAL IS INFINITE

We may
encounter many
defeats but we
must not be
defeated.

Maya Angelou

You are ready
and able to do
beautiful things
in this world.

Jim Carrey

You deserve
to feel great
about yourself

I am my own
experiment.
I am my own
work of art.

Madonna

Beware;
for I am fearless,
and therefore
powerful.

Mary Shelley

Be you, and be relentlessly you.

Lady Gaga

YOU'RE
THE BEST

Have you enjoyed this book?
If so, find us on Facebook at
Summersdale Publishers, on Twitter
at **@Summersdale** and on Instagram
at **@summersdalebooks** and get in
touch. We'd love to hear from you!

www.summersdale.com

YOU'RE
THE BEST